CW00499067

# The Tattooist's Chair

Smokestack Books
1 Lake Terrace, Grewelthorpe, Ripon HG4 3BU
e-mail: info@smokestack-books.co.uk
www.smokestack-books.co.uk



ISBN 978-0-9955635-8-2

Smokestack Books is represented
by Inpress Ltd

# The Tattooist's Chair

Karl Riordan

Smoke Stack Books

# Contents

## Mirror, Signal, Manoeuvre

I watch through the chink in the bedroom door,
my father slicks back his interlocking D.A.
Three angled mirrors at the dressing table
as he whistles to *Lipstick on your Collar*.
The crackling record spins in the corner,
grooved like his black Brylcreemed hair.

Listen to the rumpus, the fumbling upstairs,
slotting his record collection into boxes
unaware of me pacing below.
I catch him at the front door
as he tries to make a quick getaway,
a day I'd been expecting.

He drives off in his blue Datsun Cherry
leaving me straddling the white line.
Then the gear crunch at the end of the road,
and you can *bet your bottom dollar*
that he's checking his rear view mirror.

## Stag's Head

How it made its way into our living room
left me flummoxed.
The nostrils were the barrels of a gun,
its eyes fixed upon us.
It let me stroke the snout smooth
and dark as a bowling wood.
Antlers held up the roof of that house.
When I came home it was gone
leaving a shield-shaped mark.
My father in his drunkard's sleep,
wedding ring laid beside his bruised head
like the start of a thought bubble.

Then in the Scottish bed and breakfast,
twenty odd years on,
another stag hanging in reception
looking down at this young couple
signing the same surname for the first time.
The landlady starts to show us around
stopping off first in the lounge.
I hear snoring behind the settee.

## Grouse Farm

The bodhrán is a full moon in his lap,
a banjo fingered like a hot panhandle.
We've brought the smell of cold into the room,
our boots still claggy from the grouse farm
where we heaved up over the chained gate,
left a toe-print dented in the stirrup
of the hand-painted 'P' on the tin sign:
'Private Land. Keep Out!'
Dropping down we'd tip-toed on as trespassers
our strides shushed through knee-deep ferns,
each step sparked off grouse like fireworks.
We scratched together our own nest
hidden amongst bracken.

The fiddler's shadow casts a puppet thief,
faceless, leaving no trace of fingermarks.
You pocket change at the bar from your round,
carry equal tumblers of triples like scales.
We chink, and giggle at your choice of scotch.

## Diane's Pool Hall

After a night shift checking-in drunk guests,
I go with Felipe for breakfast, ale and pool.
We tower stack silver coins in the queue
waiting for Billy to pot the seven.
He misses and the thud of the white
rebounds around the blue baize table.
He bayonets his pal in the gut with a cue,
clack of sticks the sound of two rutting stags.
Fallujah's being bombed on mute T.V.
I tug on the cuff of my sweater
and wonder if the woman serving
is Diane and how she got into this?
Her alto voice calls to cut it out.
An old man sat nearby makes cooing sounds,
his top-set of teeth fall down in his mouth.
He extracts the grin, necks a pint of heavy.
Billy-boy sinks the black ball like a gulp.

—

## Peter & Joyce

She once heard tattoos etch down to the bone;
his fingers and thumb laid-out like typebars,
the raised blue scars before her spelling out
*Pete* and *Joyce* as if to print the white shroud.

Shift back: raven beehive, dark shades
and that polka-dot scarf snatched away,
by the wind of 1961 on Scarborough pier.
A weekend away bound under fake names
entered into the visitors book – a smile.

Our last day you offered your hands forward,
white-knuckled at the buzz of the gun.
Through a chink I watched your moist face flinch
and waited quiet in the parlour room.
The drive back – up front – I studied your hands
clenched again, red-raw, steering us home.

## The Price of Coal

Who'd have thought my Uncle Pete on the box?
First screening we filled the sofa, I'm crammed
between Dot and Joyce trying to spotlight
a son, husband, father, now an extra.
He plays his everyday life, wired, on call
for the Yorkshire Mines Rescue Service.
Years of searching, I found the film online
and snapped it up as a memorial,
I never attended the funeral.

It wasn't long after his cremation,
me and Mam are perched on separate chairs.
Underground scene's like a radio show,
she strains to pick out his voice, moves closer
to the screen rather than use the remote.
Hands sift through coal, props, someone moans below.
We're still in the dark until: *That's our Pete!*
Then we find his appearance and freeze-frame.
Action: rise from the cage, seconds squinting
he takes the dead-weight of the stretcher.

She makes me rewind to her brother's shot,
he hauls the limp corpse back into the lift
bouncing between their grip like 'bumps' at school.
He tears the blanket off like a plaster
the soaked, poppy patch dries to grey marl.
Cage doors are yanked shut in silent rattle,
they are gulped back down the winding shaft.
Why does she press me to play it over?

# Gallery

That day was like being held underwater;
kitted-out like Cyclops,
our battery packs threaded onto our belts,
four of us head down the mining gallery.
Our uncle made us turn off our headlamps
to consider the dark for a minute.
He tried to spook us about a lost miner –
Trapped Harry – mouth stuffed with fallen coal dust.
Then Pete's head switched-on to up-light his face,
a scream, an open gob roared, spoke of fire.

# Feathers

I kept finding these feathers in the lawn,
seemed I was the only one to notice.
It was every morning alike, these quills
spiked in the grass, thought I was losing it.
Then last Saturday I opened my purse
to pay-off the butcher; a fine white one
there in the pouch, it nearly knocked me down.
I gripped in case I dominoed the queue.

Then I heard about this spiritualist,
had to book up two months in advance
for a reading at her kitchen table,
said I ought to come with an open mind –
could even have it on tape. I mean, who else
could I tell about these feathers from heaven?

# Bulbs

It took some thought to mark out the circle.
He'd become a rooting noise from the garage,
surfaced with twine, a stake and aerosol.
She caught the thud as the mallet hit home –
his centre point.
He started to rotate anti-clockwise
and left himself marooned on his island,
looking back at her framed in the window.

The sudden interest in gardening,
at all hours, left her flummoxed
and despite the rasp of his chest
he'd made a raised bed ready for the bulbs.

When the hospice called she'd just left him,
with new socks knitted with days of the week,
had to pull onto the hard shoulder.

Spring, amongst the colour-coded patch,
she had to blink, twice.
Her eyes pick out violet blooms spelling:
*Peter* and *Joyce.*

## St Francis in a Sheffield Pet Shop

A child runs his fingers along the bars
like playing glissando on piano.
St Francis frowns at the young lad,
his fingernails the length of talons
tap the boy's collarbone that rings hollow
and he flees downstairs out into the street.
Alone with his sisters the birds
the cockatoo screams for attention.
Francis looks into the cage,
the quiet is ringing.
It's white head tilts to one side,
the crest feathers raise to a Mohawk.
Peach faced lovebirds hop perch
to perch and back again.
The mirror is a framed disk
and our saint knows the 50-60
heart beats per minute are being wasted
quick as a tick of a wristwatch.
But it's the Zebra Finch that makes him weep,
pecking at its feathers
it looks out with streaming Mascara eyes.
The urge to unhitch coop doors
he imagines reaching up to the elbow,
being on a spot-lit stage drum roll
confetti of birds from conjurer's cuff.

## Docking

We were about to land
on the banks of the Clyde.
Two older lads –
probably now in their fifties –
threw their coats overboard.
One lit two cigarettes in his mouth,
passed a fag over to his pal
then checked his inner wrist for the time.
In school books drawing the Saltire
without lifting from the paper;
the *Zorro* 'Z' turns into an envelope.
The nib split like my father's fingernail
pressing onto the road atlas, *Bellshill* –
the car radio changing accents.

I never found out why their Parkas
got tossed into the black water;
as if casting nets for something
or shedding their outer shells,
if they left anything in their pockets.

# Finsbury Park, London, 1961

*after Don McCullin*

Eddie lifted his foot onto the chipped chair,
shoes buffed the colour of that full rum bottle
sat on the makeshift games table.
We'd brought our furniture out to the yard.
I'd just shorn my brother's hair tight,
the clippings of his afro blew away
through London backstreets
like tumbleweed.
This England was warming up,
us three prepared to drink and gamble.
We matched up the pips of dominoes,
the knocks on Formica getting harder, louder.
Then we'd mix-up the numbers,
talk about Jamaica and 'tip-over' points.
It brought my woman out to click her tongue
wafting away 'Player's Navy Cut' smoke,
snatching our washing to fold and straighten.
Then Benny tried to spook us,
fell backwards onto a chatter of bottles.
Days later my head stretches the crew neck
of that smoked tee-shirt into a new world.

## Paternoster

We hop on at ground level and ascend
hand in hand
all the way to the eighteenth
to play in the clouds
and look out to Neepsend.
Like someone threading the rosary
going round on the Hail Mary's.
At the fourteenth to sixteenth
I went past, hair all Vaselined,
to all mussed up.
We turn at the top
as if moving on a blueprint.
On the way down like a morning
in a pit shaft
where language changes from home.
You step out at the mezzanine
leaving me to keep sinking
past ground to basement
with a split decision, where to get off.

## Fourteen Powell Street

Cabbage Whites were everywhere that summer,
my father framed in a JCB cab
drives three quarters up the narrow terraced row,
fetching neighbours out to their doorsteps.
Hands push lever to bucket scrape,
concrete blocks thud into sludge
colonising our front garden.

My back once pressed against upturned hardness
like the corner of a boxing ring.
I'm hiding after the street watched me fight
and lose to fifteen year old Mavis.
My eye turned to a closed mussel shell.

The street sign they forgot to remove still stands
leading to what's left to the imagination.
Homes now vanished
but amongst scrubland are those slabs
like a memorial, they make me blush.

## My Old Flower

So there I was the other day chasing
Charlie Williams through the Barnsley precinct.
He dribbled his way through shoppers, a spin
on the heel, eyes forward he kept a straight line
parting crowds like Moses and the sea.
I held my distance, noticed folk nod, point.
Haven't you learnt to live with this by now?
The distance between us was constant,
like the north-north field of a magnet.
He noticed my reflection in Greenwood's
shop window, I looked down,
appearing interested in a tuxedo.
*Tha'll look smashing in that my old flower.*
He always had the last laugh did Charlie.

# The Dabbity

James drove over the border with presents;
hugging the white line, he took the road south
leaving behind Tunnock's factory girls
going dotty over marshmallow rows.

That night laughter filtered through floorboards
jigging-it around my bed.
He insisted on retiring after midnight,
climbing up to his curtain drawn cab.

Over that weekend we sat at the wheel,
I eyed the rubber King-Kong we'd won
at the fair, bungee hung from his mirror.
His greased kiss-curl kept falling
as we loud-mouthed to Be Bop A Lula.

The last day he bought me a dabbity;
spat on the back of my hand,
'press the transfer, two minutes, peel slowly'
revealing a sweated Chinese dragon.

By Monday it cracked to a snakeskin patch
visible enough for Mr Malkin
to point out, scrub red-raw over the sink.
I kept the word tucked under my tongue,
wafer thin, it dissolved into my body.

# After School and Weekends

Aggie fussed in and out of the kitchen,
bringing in floppy bread and butter.
The tension built up on Saturdays,
she'd wear her pinny with pockets so deep
she could pick out a wish by fingertip.
I'm perched on the black-leaded shelf,
back pressed against the oven.
Crowds start to boo from the tele
as Giant Haystacks stomps into the ring
and we all hope he'll fall through.
Big Daddy fetches a stadium roar,
his sequinned leotard catches the light.
Aggie, rocking in her chair now,
shreds the *Radio Times* to coleslaw.
Andrew is cross-legged on the floor
still struggling with the hoist since age ten
when Muscular Dystrophy took hold.
His limbs are twisted in grey marl school socks
as if someone had applied heat and moulded
his ankles into hockey sticks.
He still manages to bray the floor
holding his opponent into submission
*three, two, one.*

## Make-do

Sprawled in the road like cans of spilt paint,
he wears a lime green shirt and odd socks,
the tailback getting longer.
The woman that hit him, dressed for the office
flies out of her car in stilettos
shedding her outer skin of shoulder-pads.
They slide him into the ambulance
like risen dough into an oven
then speed off with blues flashing.
Scene of Crime Officers measure angles,
chalk the street in white hyphens.
A police woman pushes castellated crowds,
her chequered hat knocked cock-eyed,
unravels the *Police Line. Do Not Cross.*
As for us on the cordoned off bus,
we have to occupy ourselves.
Teenagers grab the back seat;
pensioner up-front winds-up his radio,
Elgar bleeding out of sponge earphones.
I think of this dead boy
making-do with random socks this morning,
his mother sorting laundry months after.

## Around the Hearth at Halloween

Coals breathe, my young legs marked
with fireside-tartan blotches.
Shirt sleeves rolled-up above the elbow,
Rab slides the knife in,
flat-cap tilted back.
He scoops out the turnip's brains,
hollows out our door-to-door lantern.

The carved smile of castellated teeth
haloes residents in terraced streets.
Our unbalanced snorkel pockets
like weighing scales as we walk.
We were the shake of a tambourine.

We count-up small towers of coppers,
pick the moonlight scabs of candle wax
spattered upon our clothes and hands.
The charred lantern like a shrunken head
beside his redundant Davy Lamp.

## Playing House

*after Don McCullin*

Two shadows like oil spillages behind me
almost stepped into the photo frame.
That yard was all hopscotch, scribble, wire,
that tailed off into our outside lavvy.

I'm still clean in my Sunday dress –
braided hair, not nappy.
A thin rope is my necklace of pearls,
footed in mother's heels I grow inches.
The sun streaks through the lattice fence
branding X's on my legs.
I cradle my white doll, Flo, to my chest;
watch the working eye wink when I rock
and tuck her into the buckled pram.

That toe dented metal bin – tilted lid,
beside un-mortared bricks we had to trust.
A bucket full of water stands
by my imagined letterbox,
'just in case'
I also have a fire-rag posted.
Those steps, bolted gate, the Anansi man.

## Made from Girders

*Edinburgh International Airport*

Straight-backed and perched on high stools,
Dougie and his son share drinks
in the departure lounge bar
before flying to their new home.

Dad clicks open a can of Irn-Bru
and the ginger fizz skooshes out,
a last swallie on birth soil,
a take-away feeling in the gut.

Up in the air Scottish bubbles
will shoogle in their stomachs,
a fruity belch of rusty water
bellowed from the boy's breath.

The father recalls Formica tables,
his mother's head parcelled up in a scarf.
How she scolded him that time
for his rudeness in the café,

then licked her pocket hanky
and thumbed the corner of his mouth
like sticking postage stamps,
shaping the lips he sees on his child.

## Tarzan

Knee deep in fronds making my own path
towards the 'Tarzan' swing, hung like a plumb
bob and line dropped from the cool canopy.
Lasers of sunlight mottle the ground.
Initials carved into calloused bark,
I span years when we played in this spot,
finger the letters of my young hand.

We lit a fire, roasted potatoes
stolen from the stall of Dunn's corner shop.
On leaf moss we talked and swigged warm cider,
faces reddening close to the ashes.

I scramble up the eroding bank,
thread the watch-chain stick between my legs,
and let go leaving something of myself
as sideways I am flung out to sketch an arc
then spin like a sycamore seed.

Walking through the backdoor of my mother's
she notices moist red mud on my knees
*Your dinner's in the oven, we've had ours.*

# These days

my sleep is one eye open,
quick as a National cash till total.

I can't stop thinking
*and all the times I had the chance to.*

Two things or is that three?
Maybe fractions, moving decimal points

like stab marks between my brother's fingers
splayed flat on the kitchen table

as he recounts why he's on the loose,
himself with the threat of Dupuytren's

Contracture – hands clawed like a gunslinger –
passed down two generations we know of.

I wake myself running through wheat crops,
my dog lolling in the chair, following.

## Recipe

Back from fishing he's upstairs tipping
live eels into a full bath,
writhing into figures of eight.
Listen to him cursing with the thud
of the fisherman's priest dashing down.

Mags is frying onions for his Dublin Coddle –
handkerchief optional.
Sear the pork until browned,
mix with stock,
carrots and layered potatoes.
Bring to a simmer,
sprinkle with ground glass.
Leave to stew until meat is tender
or crabbit husband clatters home from pub.
Stir occasionally, season to taste.
She flinches at his reflection
over her shoulder combing up his hair,
unlit cigarette attached to his lips,
zipped up jacket sounds the only farewell.
Down the path he turns up his collar,
pushes the gate outwards into the street
like swinging into a Western saloon.

Sit the supper tray onto his lap,
place remote into open palm,
quietly pull the ball-catch on the door.

## Road to Nowhere

Barney perches on the caravan steps,
drinks tea from a dented enamel mug,
stares at a scribble of hawthorn hedge
as nest-making sparrows flit out and in.

Brida washes crockery and trinkets,
hands them down to her children.
They wrap up pots in local press headlines,
stow away heirlooms and the old lies.

A police helicopter strims the air;
their Virgin Mary trembles, looks skywards
from the garden patch. A boy cries
as their blue balloon is sucked away.

The sticks of foxed placards rattle
against the disconnected
gas bottles. *Stop Evicshen.*
*Let our Childran go to School.*

## Admiral

Call it what you want, you'll find me today
at the bar in the *Admiral Duncan.*
Fidgeting, I wait for another bevy,
chat to the Italian barman
who susses I'm not a regular –
fine by him.
He lifts my glass, wipes Olympic rings clean.

Polari spat from the table for two
*Don't tell me 'bout last Wednesday,*
*out trolling on me tod,*
*approached by this chicken*
*only out for a doss.*

Wind back, '99, David Copeland
perched on a stool, day off from work
fretting at being recognised in these parts.
He's planned his exit, leaving behind news
yet to be yelled by street vendors.
Ill weather zipped in a holdall.

The surgeon will hold up to the light
a quicksilver x-ray of a baby,
head bowed,
embedded nail in the skull,
a lightning bolt.

# Eggs

I'd shed the warm duffle coat at the gate,
roll and stash it under the privet
to reveal my black satin bomber jacket.
I'd cream off my week's dinner money
to be made dizzy on the waltzer,
or watch operators walk the boards
on the cocks and hens.
Teenagers would chat over the music
shielded hands and puffs of smoke
like napkin rings.
Then that one time I got an offer
to share a ride on the eggs
by an older guy from school.
Part of the thrill was to pause
at the top and rock the cage
until it would overturn
as if being rolled down a hill.
It was the fingerless gloves
spelling *Nick Kershaw*
knitted across his knuckles
that I noticed in the air.
My thought was with my rolled
coat, I hoped would still be there.

## Simple Pleasures

There's a smell of stale beer and salty crisps,
horses race on the television screen,
newspapers spread out like maps
with contagious red penned circles.
Dennis has his top-set
placed beside his pint of Mackeson,
his gums smooth as melted plastic,
a laugh like a baby's rattle.

My father takes me to The Tollgate,
eight years old, drinking bitter shandy.
Bill Kirk has handed over
a 1940's Bush radio in a bin liner.
I unwrap the square to its blonde leather finish,
twist the dial from Hilversum to Eireann
as if counting stops on a railway track.
They tell me, *it only plays old time music.*
Our dog circles around my dad's leg
nudging into his calf, blue veined
tattooed with nicks of coal only I know.

Today, it's the tang of grease and builder's dust,
as on dad's hands that makes this mixture mine.
His flannel work slacks flecked with concrete
from the slap and tamp of unset warehouse floors.
This is why, of late, I sit in certain pubs.

# When Summer Came

Five full months we'd worked together on sites,
Phil taught me how to drive the dumper truck.
At midday he'd bought me a pint of bitter,
told sex stories and about growing-up.
At sixteen, I followed in his size ten boot prints
like a scene-of-crime plaster cast.
He turned in for work one morning, head skinned,
by afternoon the sun had seared his neck red.
In unison, the slap of timber tamp
stipples over the thick, unset concrete.
We rest partway; he peels off his t-shirt,
SKREWDRIVER tattoos his off-white chest.
I can no longer look him in the eye
and from then on we see-saw out-of-step.

## Oaklands

Stacked crutches pressed against the window pane,
oxter pads the colour of worn plasters.
Mr Bell will be propped up in bed now
shouting in his room at *Match of the Day*.

Tomorrow we'll skid on studs to the park;
he'll be in director's chair, chewing gum,
sat in the foyer of the old folks' home.
He'll stop us and we'll test him for toffees,
try to trip him up as he tallies
any football club to their home turf.
A pen tapping seconds on the chair arm.
A click of finger and thumb:
*The Dell*
    *Easter Road*
*Anfield*
    *Oakwell.*

When he doesn't show in the entrance
of his own dug-out, we press the buzzer
and a care assistant invites us in.
We unlace a boot, hop, do it again
feel the weft of the carpet.
She asks us to sign the visitors' book.
While I'm tying knots with my signature
there's no time to dot
– we're ushered down a corridor.
We pass Mrs Simmons trying to find
the end of the skirting board with her stick,
*my boys, my lovely boys.*

In his room the bed is stripped.
*He insisted you have these:* old programmes,
tickets and a spot-the-ball coupon
of pixellated footballers mid air.
They crane for the nought of a missing ball,
his biro prints had scored a crown of kisses.

## Man in a Barn

*after the death of Joe McDonnell, Long Kesh, 1981*

Hunched forward on a bale of hay, Tomás
smudges his fingerprints from each red bead
like lowering a pail into a well.
The Velcro sound of his facial stubble
doesn't trouble him now.
High shadow sidling up, stench of horse
he cannot command anymore.
Pulling off his shoes they are flung
left, right, through the upper stable door.

Staring out to the farthest field
he draws a grey blanket tight
over his head like a hermit.
Rosary snaps around his dirty fist
onto the cobbled courtyard outside,
the tinkle of pills dropping in a sink.

## Stars

I am sat at the table with Kieran,
helping him make a spyglass
out of cardboard toilet roll holders.
I keep the scissors out of his reach
but let him hold two tubes in place
while I wind tape around clockwise.
*We've got enough to see into the future.*

Will he focus on the way he'll fold his suit,
lining up the creases of his trousers
before having to feel his way around her,
listening to tomorrow's bus fare drop
onto the floor of a darkened lodging room?

Or the way he'll walk past his door
counting up loose change, whistling
past two braying heavies and a suit,
have to push himself through the back privet
getting his *best fucking jacket* snagged?

The pans he'll have to scrub 'til breathless,
stealing one piece of cutlery each day,
slipping a point of Sheffield Steel up t'cuff
or the time he'll explode at the funeral
for the priest referring to his mother as *Dot.*

Talking of dots, we couldn't skip over
the art room and the way Indian ink
will blemish his knuckles like dice pips,
tugging cuffs years later at interview
pinned to the wall by a panel of *twats.*

He'll get a laugh in the assembly hall though,
as his hand slips through the neck hole
of an emu glove-puppet, poking through the curtain
behind the headmaster and police officer,
addressing cross-legged children
drawing snakes and spots on their mate's back.

Maybe he'll find his girl held by another,
at nearly thirty he might climb up trees
shouting out at her, never to be heard.
I know that echo can last for years.
I offer glue and silver glitter
but Kieran whacks his telescope in two.

## Button It

My brother, Christmas Eve turning midnight.
On my sofa he's tucked-in at the neck,
in-hiding, a warrant out for his arrest,
doped on Temazepam, street name - Green Eggs.
He's damp with the smell of rain,
roughing it up from Hitchin.
Teeth the colour of broken walnuts
but it's his bleach blonde hair that gets me,
yellow twisted tendrils - still gelled.
On the radio Elvis sings, *In The Ghetto*
bringing back mornings my mother parted
his downy hair, buttoned up his duffle,
thumbing the toggle at his throat
before sending him off on the school route.
The coat got rolled, stuffed under privet,
then off to feed dinner money into slots,
tapping flashing buttons,
trying to predict the reels of ripe fruit.
It paid out one Friday,
dropping the seventy pound jackpot - twice.
I knew then he'd keep on pushing his luck.

## Counting on our fingers

Our hands are quite alike;
a talking point in later years
for those silences over a pint.

*Dupuytren's Contracture,*
the doctor told my father.
His little finger tightly curled
like a punctured party streamer.

I compared our hands in your JCB.
Secretly watched you jerk the levers,
a clutch of half sucked Kojak lollies.

The chevron tyre tracks we left behind
patterned the sludge like herringbone,
tamped down and set under concrete floors.

You lifted me down from high steps,
I clung to your bristled neck.
We were the sound of Velcro unfastening
as you placed me onto solid ground.

We meet these days attempt a manly clasp,
but that twisted digit pokes my palm
like the wrong piece of a jigsaw.

# Beachcombing

It's the only thing left of that day
when we picked ourselves up,
drove to the edge of North Berwick.

I crouched to pick limpets
like knee scabs you couldn't leave alone.
It was you who found the albino sea star
without life in a rock pool,
wanted to take it home
as if you might be able to bring it back.

I straightened up from my haunches
fourteen years on.
The starfish has hardened
to white ceramic
like the stretched hand of a pianist
playing minor arpeggios
and I silently stroke its purlicue.

## Edinburgh tenements

The inch short, petticoat lace, curtain lifts
to the rattle of the back sash-window;
calls me from a sprung bed to view the day.
So, hobbling on my yellow heels I go
to peek out to the communal backyard.

An empty child's swing pushed by the wind
regular as a pendulum.
My eyes scan two down and three across,
a women balancing her head on fists
stares out, searching for a clue.

The boy next door shoots out from the alley,
zipped up and blinkered in a snorkel coat.
He claps his hands to the sky
releasing a thousand birds.

I release my palm from the pane
watch my wafer fingerprints fade.

## Segs

I'd not heard the sound of Blakey's segs
for coming up to near thirty years.
Hammered in at the heel like horseshoes,
a pit-pony clopping
down the school corridor.
Friday afternoon, double maths, mocks.
Three months into the strike,
counting what we didn't have.
Sullivan entered the classroom late,
the stink of diffs in his jacket pocket
as he was placed next to me in class.
Two-tone Sta-Press trousers,
legs outstretched and crossed,
the iridescence of a peacock.
Hauled up to the headmaster's office
for saying what we were not allowed to ask.
He wrote the word in his lined jotter,
slid it across the desk for me to peek.
It's been closed all this time. Open up.
Read.

## Frank's Haircut

In the council outhouse
a click of clippers
breaks the silence.

As next door neighbours
it was convenient for Frank
and pin-money for me.

This time an early cut,
wanting to look tidy
for Lilian's funeral.

The metal teeth grind
shearing away his grey fuzz
*Down to the bone.*

Then scissor over comb
I notice the coal-dust scar
tattooed on his temple.

Lifting the layers to be shorn,
his scissor-happy wife's last trim shows
and it's difficult to straighten up.

I brush away snipped whiskers
that stick and itch
like crawling corn flies.

He scatters his locks into the fire,
the singed hair fizzes away in a flash.
Into my palm he presses two pound coins.

## Sabong

Two cocks strut the dust,
scratching their marks in circles,
tied to a mini stake maypole.

Dual owners crouch,
clutching their birds
that dot, dot dash each other.
One, beak dipped in gold,
another's wattle shivers.

From a red velvet lined case,
tari are polished with a white cloth
as if laying royal cutlery.

Gaffs wound like a yo-yo
to the left leg – the reaper
our man Rogelio calls out.

*Sa pula, sa puti*
cry the Kristos
arms crucified
reeling off odds from memory.

They burst into flames
and behind the bars,
notes are counted out
like tossed feathers –
a winner fans himself.

## The Hour before Calling

This steamed pub with window smileys crying;
an elderly couple, young to each other
place their telescopic umbrellas
by the fireside, one pink another black.

His, a pirate's hook digging a way out
from an x-marks-the-spot.
Hers is a gear stick pushed into first
and I watch them huddling the blaze, blushing.

Note the wedding band has seared his finger,
hers are all costume, displayed on his right thigh.
I'm left smoking at the door as they leave,
spinning the spine of one umbrella.

## Setting Fire

I'd notice first, amber balls of your heels
as you scrunched up old news
on bitter mornings,
planting gossip into the grate.

Criss-cross the kindling,
build up the foundations
then strike a light.
The Swan burns down too close
and you flap your fingers;
flecks of paper moths
spiral up the flue.
Scraps of tittle-tattle ash,
scattered over terraces.

A double page of yesterday's runners
draws the fire to a roar,
scorching winners and losers
to a late October leaf.
As flames take hold
shadows dance round the walls.

At twelve and three quarters
I wanted to escape this place,
but you always caught me
with a finger print smudge
of coal-dust
on the tip of my nose,
marking me for days to come.

# The Barrow Seven

*'The most disastrous colliery accident which had occurred in the immediate vicinity of Barnsley for almost a generation past, has unhappily to be recorded. The scene was at the Barrow Colliery, Worsbro', where a cage mishap of an extraordinary nature resulted in seven men being hurled to the bottom of the shaft and instantaneously killed.'*
*Barnsley Chronicle*, 23 November 1907

*'...the officials speedily descended by another shaft. Here they met a horrible sight, the seven men being found lifeless, a mass of mangled humanity.'*
*Yorkshire Post*, 16 November 1907

## Thomas William Jennings

*Haulage Lad, aged 18*

*'Thomas Jennings stated that his lad had worked in the pit about four years. He was insured. Witness produced for the Coroner's inspection the watch which his son was wearing at the time of the accident. It was in a celluloid case, and had apparently suffered no injury beyond the breaking of the glass. The hands had stopped at ten minutes past four.'*
*Barnsley Chronicle*, 23 November 1907

had a key to number 2 Powell Street,
where I watched my Grandad hollow out turnip brains,
carve Halloween faces to shrunken heads
that became lanterns we swung door to door,
like Davy lamps, along terraced rows.

That ignored chapping
for trick or treat sweeties,
like the tap, tap
of the 'Knocker-upper'
at the bedroom window, 1907.

Tom props up his pillow;
rests back and lights a nipped Woodbine diff,
he exhales and stares at distempered walls,
notes the fading rattle of sash frames
then smiles at his snap-time joke on 'Slack-Adams'.

He tries hard not to be a 'lig-in-bed'
but slinks back under the six blankets.
His father's celluloid cased watch points out
two hours to go until he'll inhale dawn air,
shadowed by the towering winding wheels.

## The Cake

*Isaac Farrer, Haulage Man, aged 20*

Mother ruffled up my hair today
as she scuffled around the kitchen
in preparation for my 21st.
One more shift,
before reaching my *majority.*
Nothing is said only knowing looks,
keeping me out of the way, slapping hands.
My boots are unlaced warming by the fire,
just like those mornings before school.
She's blind to me lifting the oven latch
to peek and inhale the sweet smell of sponge
taking the air from the sinking cake.

## William Adams

*Brakesman, aged 28*

They nailed his father's nickname as a child,
'Slack Adams.'
Carrying that name like a crucifix pick
over his shoulder into the dark.
In secret he liked to paint,
building up the layers of oil
like coal.

As we knit along he's on guard
against Jennings' joke
sipping on a flask of water.
I overhear that name called on Barnsley market
a hundred years after.

# Tom Rathmell Cope

*Hanger-On, aged 23*

*Mrs Sarah Cope, who was weeping bitterly, said that her husband was killed at the Swaithe Main Colliery, a mile and a half away from the Barrow pit, 16 years ago. Her son had worked at Barrow since he was 13 years of age, and was her chief support. He said "Good morning, mother," at half-past five on Friday morning...'*
*Barnsley Chronicle*, 23 November 1907

He's framed, resting on the stable door
this morning, thinking about their wedding
scheduled for Christmas – auspicious.
He listens to the sparrows, how his mother
thought it lucky to awake
hearing birdsong on the big day.
*Look at the sun when you leave for the church*
*and your children will be beautiful.*
Before locking up and leaving
he stands at the foot of the stairs,
shouts up,
'Good morning, mother.'
Whistles on the way to work.

## Walter Lewis Goodchild

*Hanger-on, aged 35*

Polished like brown saddle leather, the penny
he left under the pillow for his lad.
The tooth had been loose for days
and the night time groans
would stir him to nudge Lizzy
to tend to the child
and avoid a chorus.
Then yesterday, between forefinger
and thumb it took some fiddling
to loop string to incisor,
leading twine to door handle.
The fourth attempt pulled it
followed by a shrill scream
that would ring through the house for weeks.

## Byas Rooke

*Haulage Man, aged 22*

'*Rooke happened to be amongst the ill fated party by pure chance. He had intended coming out of the seam with his brother on the previous ascent of the cage, but stopped behind to talk to a friend, saying he would come up with the next draw.*'
*Barnsley Chronicle*, 23 November 1907

My brother hooked his knap-sack around my neck
as if awarding me a fucking medal,
then pulled out his snap-tin to take a snack
of half-finished bread and jam.
I told him, *Tha's too much rattle thee,*
wanting to talk football to his mucker.

I step up onto the cage,
leave him dawdling underground
nattering like an old woman.
His face watching me ascend the shaft,
we're two coins rubbing in a waist-coat pocket.
I leave pit-talk at the gate,
off home, where I have to guard my language.

## Frank Dobson

*Chargeman, aged 40*

They laid you out on the billiard table
of the Mason's Arms.
You'll not remember, now, that time
you pocketed the cue ball
for your potty.
Then you took to shaping your own
to the size of a pigeon's egg,
insisted upon an upturned Grimethorpe brick
to rest and chip the nipsy
waist height, then thwack the ovoid
to the back of beyond.
That park I went along to watch
you in the act, the rise allowed seven times
then your long knock.
Of late, I walk the perimeter of the field,
listening for the clack of a hickory stick.

# Notes

## The Price of Coal

The Price of Coal was a two-part BBC television drama written by Barry Hines and directed by Ken Loach, first broadcast on 29 March, 1977

## My Old Flower

The title was the catchphrase of Charlie Williams, a miner, professional footballer and stand-up comedian. He has been praised by some and criticized by others for his racial stereotyping of black people.

## The Dabbity

The title comes from a Scottish word for a temporary, stick on tattoo often sold to children.

## Road to Nowhere

The inspiration for this stems from the eviction of the Dale Farm Travellers evicted from their land.

## Sabong

*Sabong* is the Tagalog word for cockfighting. The *Kristos* take the bets, so called because his posture of extended arms resembles Christ nailed on the cross. *Sa pula, sa puti* translates as for the red rooster, for the white rooster. *Tari* are the spurs bound to the legs of the cock.

## The Barrow Seven

Nipsy is an old South Yorkshire game using a brick, potty or nipsy and a stick; the aim is to clip the nipsy with a stick and hit it as far as possible. It has been called 'miner's golf.'